A Little Book
About

Me
and my
Mom

Illustrated by Jedda Robaard

BARRON'S

This is a book to fill in and share with your mom.
You may need some help to complete it — that's what moms are for!
You can use the pouch in the back of the book to store photographs,
postcards, birthday cards, and anything else that is special to you and your mom.
Write a special message for your mom in the gift card provided.

First Edition for North America published in 2014
by Barron's Educational Series, Inc.

Copyright © The Five Mile Press Pty Ltd, 2013
Illustrations © Jedda Robaard

First published in 2013 by
The Five Mile Press Pty Ltd
1 Centre Road, Scoresby
Victoria 3179 Australia
www.fivemile.com.au
Part of the Bonnier Publishing Group
www.bonnierpublishing.com

All inquiries should be addressed to:
Barron's Educational Series, Inc.
250 Wireless Boulevard
Hauppauge, NY 11788
www.barronseduc.com

ISBN: 978-0-7641-6671-6

Library of Congress Control No.: 2013949687

Date of Manufacture: November 2013
Manufactured by: Leo Paper Products Ltd, Kowloon, Hong Kong, China.

Product conforms to all applicable CPSC and CPSIA 2008 standards.
No lead or phthalate hazard.

Printed in China
9 8 7 6 5 4 3 2 1

This is my
mom
and **me**.

Draw or attach a photo of
you and your mom here.

Mom was born in

....

Now she lives in

....

Mark these places on the map.

My mom's mom

is named

....

She is my grandma!

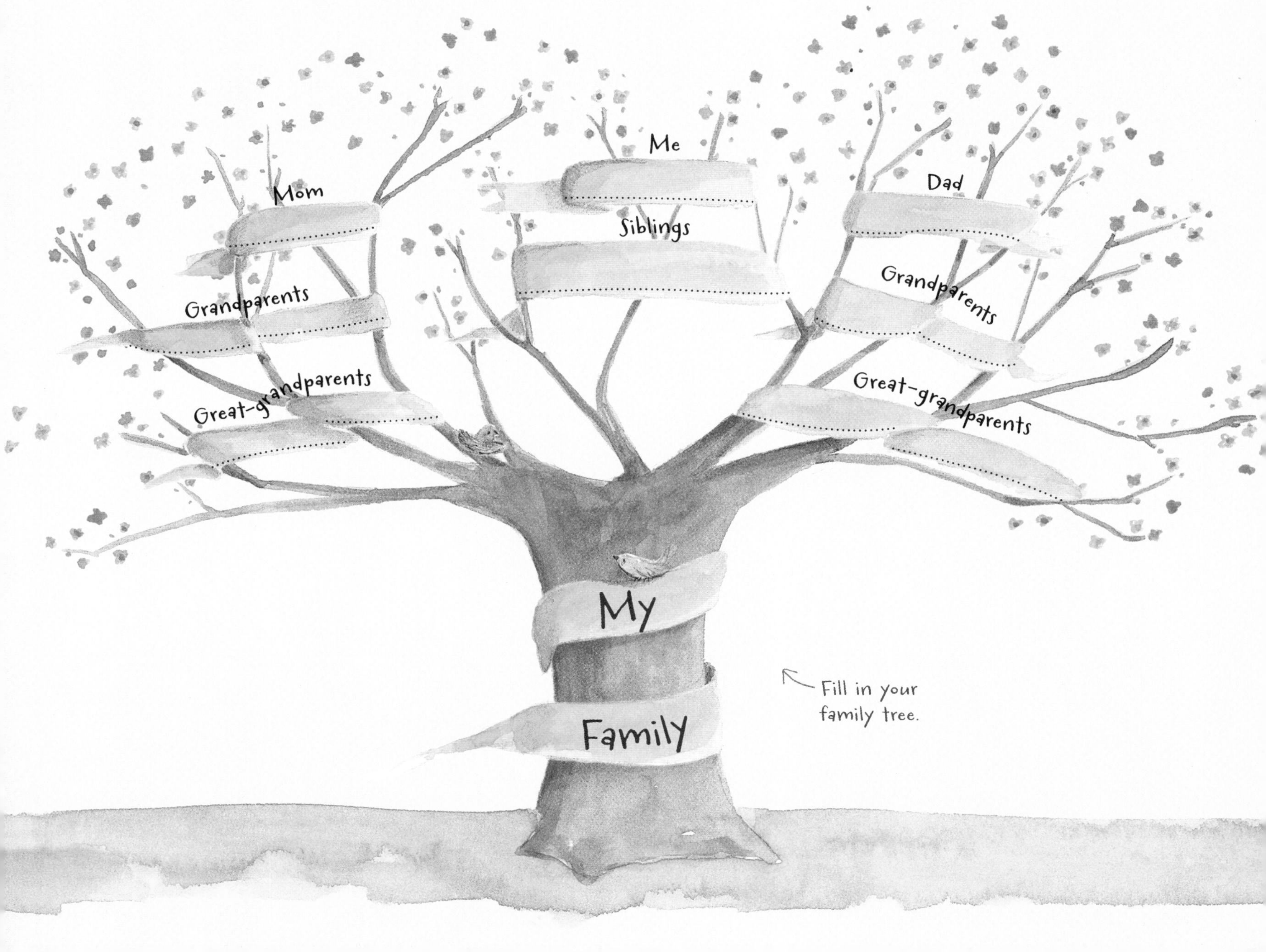

Mom

Me

Dad

Siblings

Grandparents

Grandparents

Great-grandparents

Great-grandparents

My

Family

Fill in your
family tree.

When
Mom
was little,

her favorite pastime was

....

My favorite pastime is

....

Mom and I love
trying new things.
Our favorite thing to
do together is

....

....

When Mom was young,

she had a pet ....

named ....

I have a pet ....

named ....

Our pets never met — but here is
a picture of both of them!

Draw a picture of your pets here. ↑

When Mom was my age,

she wanted to be a

....

When I grow up, I want to be a

....

Here is a picture of my mom dressed as a ....

She looks pretty / happy / funny / brave!

Draw a costume on your mom.

When Mom was young,

her favorite music was ....

Now she likes to listen to ....

My favorite music is ....

Mom's favorite
color is

....

My favorite
color is

....

Here is a painting in our favorite **colors**

Color in the painting. ↗

Mom and I love to eat yummy food.

Our favorite foods are

Make a list or draw your favorite foods here. ↗

My mom loves going on vacations.

Her favorite vacation was

....

She has always wanted to go to

....

Draw or attach a photo of you and your mom on vacation.

The **best** place Mom and I have been together is ....

For my birthday,
Mom
likes to take me to the

Mom's birthday is

..... / ..... / .....

....

The best thing we have
done together on my birthday is

....

My favorite birthday present
from Mom was

....

My
birthday is

...../...../.....

I love my mom

That's why I've made this special book and card just for her!